Love Me For Me

Author

Shabarbara Best- Everette

Love Me For Me

Words From The Heart Publishing Company books may be ordered through booksellers or by contacting:
Words From The Heart Publishing Company
www.AuthorShabarbara.com

Words From The Heart Publishing Company

Dedicated to My Inspiration, My Son

Malachi, I Will ALWAYS Love You!!!

Don't hate me because I'm brown
I have so much to offer
You'll see, if you just stick around

Take the time to get to know me
Instead of judging me because of who you
think I *might* be

My skin doesn't fully define who I am
How would you feel if I judged you Sir or
Ma'am

I already know that it would make you feel
pretty bad
When it happens to me, I always feel really
sad

You may be scared of me, but I may be scared of you too
Because you're not like me and I'm not like you

We are all different and that's okay
But I shouldn't worry about who will bully
me from day to day

People used to ask me, "Are you mixed?
Why do you have curly hair?"
No, I'm not mixed. But I will be the first one
in the barber's chair

Any curl that popped up had to be gone as quick as possible

Because getting picked on everyday was absolutely horrible

My mom told me,
"We can't please everyone.
Our beauty starts from the inside.
So, embrace your curly hair
There's no need to try to hide."

I started loving everything about me
including my hair
And it doesn't bother me when people stare

I'm finally comfortable in my brown skin
This world can be crazy, but I know that in
the end I'll always win

It may take some time for you to see
But I promise that you will agree
That others will one day
"Love Me For Me"

The End

www.ingramcontent.com/pod-product-compliance
Lightning Source LLC
Chambersburg PA
CBHW042118040426

42449CB00002B/89